I0789269

ANOTHER ENDANGERED SPECIES

Blacks in America

Vandester J Jenkins

ANOTHER ENDANGERED SPECIES
BLACKS IN AMERICA

Copyright © 2017 Vandester J Jenkins

All rights reserved.
ISBN — 10: 1975631455
ISBN — 13: 978 - 1975631451

i

Contents

Merriam-Webster

Definition of **endangered species**

1. : a species threatened with extinction;
    1. *broadly*: anyone or anything whose continued existence is threatened

Species: a class of individuals having common attributes and designated by a common name

I am a Black American. I am your typical middle-class/working-poor American, and a citizen of the United States. I was born here and raised here. My roots run deep in the American soil. I have no clue of my distance ancestral past and am probably no different in that respect, from most Black Americans in the United States of America. Yet, as most Black Americans, I love being black and I love being American.

I did not ask to be born Black or female. I did not decide on my race or sexual origin. There was a higher power involved in that decision. But I do feel strongly that I was born a Black American female for a reason, and that my Creator knew I would be strong enough to handle it. And as Ms. India.Arie so eloquently stated, "I know my Creator didn't make no mistake on me."

So why I am dehumanized, victimized, vilified, and demonized simply because of something that I had no control over. Am I to be classified as **ANOTHER ENDANGERED SPECIES**.

CHAPTER 1

Our Own Worst Enemies

As a race of people, Black Americans have historically, been subjected to some of the worst atrocities known to man. In the past, our ancestors have been enslaved; used as the workhorse for the establishment of the New World. Our ancestors' have been the actual 'backbone' of what is the foundation of the United States of America. And throughout history, we have continued to be the pack mules for progress and change.

In the middle 1900's, marches were held so that Black Americans would be recognized as more than just the 'doormat' for others to walk on and the physical backbone of the United States, but as a very significant participant in the evolutionary progress of the USA. Yet, Black Americans have done nothing but struggle since the very beginning, and we still struggle today in 2017.

As Blacks move towards a more culturally-balanced way of life, we continue to run into activities and actions that places us against racial brick walls. These walls are not just the ones that are covert and overt by non-blacks, but ones that are subconsciously and consciously perpetrated by some of our own. We are our own worst enemies, but do we realize it?

In an effort to dehumanize blacks during slavery times, Africans that were imported to 'New World' as slaves, were subjected to the systematic division of the family unit. The main purpose of this action was to force submission and invoke mental control over slaves. To control the mind, and thereby control the body of an entire race of people. To attempt to thoroughly enslave humans, and brainwash them into believing that one race of people could completely control and manipulate another race of people. Even though separating families as they were docked on the shores of America continued throughout slavery, the cycle of separation continued on throughout time, but the attempted control of mind and body by another race did not.

Today, separation of Black families still exists to the point that we have no real familiar bonds within our race. Yes, we may have a certain level of unity for our immediate families, but we have no real clue as to who our extended family members are, or even if they exist. Yet we do very little to change that. Instead, we allow ourselves to be internally demonized by our own. In our communities, we kill off our own; when some of us gain wealth and status, we ridicule our own for not meeting the new standards; we don't support our businesses, and our businesses, in turn, over-inflate the cost of doing business within our neighborhoods and communities; we ridicule our people for talking well, and criticize those who struggle to break the 'ebonics' cycle; we terrorize our people who try to take care of their own, yet we will not approach struggling areas to help them improve; we believe that we are giving our children a better life than our own by tossing money at them, yet we don't give them enough attention and love to keep them happy and focused. We even go so far as to actively support other communities, yet impugn our own. Some of us are so clueless as to believe that bigotry and racism against Blacks does not exist, and may even go so far as to state that it is all in our 'minds'. But hardcore evidence has proven, otherwise.

   Black Americans, we are our own worst enemies. As a powerful race of people, we need to make positive changes within our own race, before anyone else will see fit to change towards us.

CHAPTER 2

Racism in the Government

Throughout my career, I have worked in some capacity within the federal government. From my personal experiences, the United States Federal Government practically lives by the moto: "Do as I say, not as I do". And what do I mean by that? Let me explain.

As a Black Female in the government, I learned early on that racism is alive and well. At every opportunity to succeed, that were even more obstacles of failure for Blacks.

My first year working for the Federal Aviation Administration (FAA) was an eye-opening experience. Because of Affirmative Action, I was able to gain a position within the Agency but there was no guarantee that I would keep it. The challenge to survive was on.

  During my first week in the agency, I was told by several Black employees that my job was going to be difficult, not because I was not physically able to perform the tasks but because I was the wrong color and gender. I was even told by a higher-level manager who was male and Caucasian, that, "You're here now, but let's see if you gonna stay." I felt that that was an odd comment to make to a new hire. I was a little skeptical at first, but found out the hard way, just how true their statements were.

I was told that there would be every obstacle placed in my way to see me fail, and they were. And those obstacles continued throughout my career, which ended in 2017, when I finally retired. No one ever stated to me directly, how bias the government would be towards Blacks, but their actions spoke volumes.

My initial training was with a gentleman who was dedicated to ensuring that I received the best training possible. He had his doubts but shared with me that, as long as I did what was needed and learned my job well, he could care less about anything else. I had nothing but respect for him. I learned much from him, and he learned to respect and understand that being Black was not a 'contagious disease' or a race of 'incompetent beings'.

As I attempted to move up the ladder, many obstacles were placed in my way. The first big obstacle was that, at the time that I came into the agency, I started with three white males and I was the only Black in this group, of any gender. This should not have been an obstacle, but it was.

We all started at the same pay grade. We each worked in different units, and our skill sets were comparable. After a couple of months, the three males were offered the opportunity to resubmit their applications for the next higher pay-grade level. No one told me. I was not even aware that they received this opportunity until someone, confidentially, informed me of what was happening. Leaving no doubt as to what was going on, I asked one of the three white males about the promotional opportunity and he confirmed it. When I asked my direct-reporting supervisor about it, he initially denied it. But when I informed him that one of the others confirmed the opportunity, he retracted his denial and allowed me to re-apply. I qualified and received the pay increase.

Next obstacle was with my formal training. I realized that everyone else was attending formal training on the 'theory of operations' of the systems and services that we were responsible for maintaining. When I requested to be provided formal training, my supervisor informed me that the training was for the journey-level technicians, only. Journey-level technicians were the specialists with senior maintenance responsibility. Because they were the lead specialists for each shift, their training needs had to be met, prior to the needs of any developmental employees. Developmental employees were basically the newly hired employees, of which I was included.

I accepted this information as fact until I became aware that the other three new-hire employees where sent away to attend training at every opportunity, as developmental technicians. Since they were given their opportunity to attend formal training, I asked for my opportunity. It was denied without a reason. Management's denial motivated me to learned the theory of operations on my own, and I trained myself on all of the systems and services that I was responsible for maintaining. I worked hard and learned every aspect of the area that I was assigned to, and some of the areas outside of my assignment. Even without the formal training, I became a 'Go-To' specialists for many critical systems. Though management attempted to deny my abilities, my skillsets were undeniable. So much so that, as a developmental technician, I was assigned a shift by my supervisor, and I worked it alone without any problems. I was even recognized for doing an exceptional job by my senior specialists. And I was also acknowledged as the first specialist to ever stand watch unsupervised, as a developmental technician.

When the time came for me to gain my next higher pay-grade level, I was deployed in the Gulf War, with Operation Desert Storm. You see, not only did I work for the Federal Government but at the time, I was also an inactive member of the United States Air Force, with nine years of prior active duty service. Upon my return from deployment, I submitted a request for my promotion. I was trained on everything and worked unsupervised, routinely, and when I returned from deployment, I stepped back into my roll as a "Go-To" specialist. I was immediately informed that, because I was away with the military, I had to wait three more months before I could be upgraded to the next pay-grade level. Even though I was trained on all of the systems and services, and certified on all the major systems and services available, the FAA did not consider me qualified to be a journey-level technician. You see, each level increase required that a technician work in the previous level for a minimum of one year. Because of my time of absence for deployment of three months, my upgrade was to be delayed for another three months.

It was not a qualification issue but a management decision, because I was more than qualified to gain the promotion. I found out later that I was the only one who had to wait after any deployment. I received a memo stating that I would not be upgraded until the three-month period was over. So, I waited.

When I finally received my higher level, I was officially able to attend formal training. Or so I thought. Once I requested to attend training, I was informed by my newest manager that the formal training was for new employees and not for journey-level employees, which I was. I was also informed that I would have to wait until slots became available, after the new hires were trained. So, I waited, again.

Eventually, I was able to finally gain the necessary training, but only through subterfuge. Though I qualified for little, in the eyes of management, I was always the one that was left in charge whenever my supervisor would take time off. So, I used my temporary status as supervisor, to my advantage. Whenever my manager took time off from work and left me in charge, I would sign myself up for any class available. It had taken him some time before he finally caught on.   But by then it was too late. I was on my way to attend formal training, finally. Even though I had the skill set to maintain all of the systems and services, credit for this training was not received without attending formal theory training. All of this impacts your performance review. My review was always low because of this.

I also experienced many issues where I would not receive credit for work that I had completed.

For example, I trained myself on a system that no one wanted to work on. I really enjoyed the work. It was challenging and stimulating. As I learned the system, I observed an anomaly that existed with the system's performance. Every now and then, an interruption would occur that caused problems with the backup path for air traffic communications. I asked if anyone knew about it and was informed that the problem had existed for about two years. I was also told that no one knew how to fix it, including the senior technicians. I found myself another challenge and took it on.

Not only did I take on the problem, I owned it. I was able to troubleshoot the system malfunction, and immediately identified the repair that was needed.   After intermittently failing for over two years, I identified and fixed the problem within a week's time frame. Because of my efforts, a tiger team was developed to go to every site along the communication's links and investigate the potential for this happening at those sites, as well as throughout the entire Agency.

I was given a verbal 'atta girl', but the senior technician received a written letter of recognition and a cash award for my work. I failed to mention that, not only was I the only female in my unit but I was also, the only Black technician in my group of approximately fifteen employees.

Another incident happened, when I was acting supervisor for a year. During that time, an investigation was initiated against my unit by the Sector Manager. During that time, many investigations were initiated and the pattern was clear – eliminate as many Blacks and females, as possible. He had previously been successfully in his elimination process but in my unit, the investigation did not turn out as the manager had hoped for.

Not only did my unit make it through the investigation but at the time, we received the best overall rating in the agency. The manager was highly disappointed in the outcome of the investigation. We did not fail in any area of the inspection, and he had finally run out of options to eliminate me from the FAA. He soon retired from the Agency. But, as with any good strategist, you ensure that you 'stack' your favorite people to leave behind a legacy of 'like' mentality. The following Sector Manager was definitely a product of the same 'mother's milk'.

After the old Sector Manager retired, I received my performance review from his replacement.

At the time, I was my unit's temporary supervisor and so I fell under his review process. The review of my performance was a true indicator of an attempt at mental submission.

At the time, performance reviews utilized an evaluation scale of '1(poor) to 10(outstanding)'. I received a 1(poor). During the face-to-face review, the manager presented me with the results and stated that that was what he observed. I didn't qualify for any better. He talked, I listened. But, at the end of the discussion, the Sector Manager made an unusual request. He asked if I would assist the 'Sector' with establishing a unique unit that would consist of two units, combined. He felt that I more than met the qualifications to handle any difficulties that the merger would create, and that I had demonstrated that I could easily handle any labor issues associated with the transition. He felt that my skills would be effective in managing both units and turning around the problems that existed, internally. ??? Though I was incredulous, I did not show any signs. I didn't even blink at the Manager. I calmly stood up, looked him in the eye, and politely informed him that, "Since I qualify so poorly in supervising one unit, per your evaluation, I definitely do not qualify to supervise two units at one time." I politely and professionally told him to get someone else to do it. Then I walked out of his office, without looking back. As far as management was concerned, I never met the qualifications to supervise on a permanent basis, and marginally on a temporary assignment. I did not receive any credit for my supervisory periods at that location for any time period of less than one year and they planned it that way. But the opportunity came for me to beat them at their own game and I did. You see, all future opportunities to temporarily supervise my unit, I respectfully declined, until an opportunity to perform the assignment for one year. I finally gained a year in the higher pay level. I could gain employment, at the next higher level, without prejudice. At least that's what I thought. But that will be discussed much later.

There was a period when our unit was establishing a new system called the 'Bandwidth Manager System(BWM)'. Another intriguing challenge for me, and I was more than ready for the opportunity.

I was so enthralled with the system's functionality, that I would spend my breaks observing its operation. During one of those periods of observance, the BWM went into full system reset. Because it was a new system within the FAA, no one was familiar with this anomaly. Even the contractor, who build the system was clueless. So, I went to work. When no one would touch the system including the contractors, I decided to make an attempt. I found that the backup processor went into 'sleep' mode and was not available for any operations. This was a design flaw. Unless defective, the processor should hold steady in the 'standby' mode. It should only go into 'sleep', when it was programmed to do so. The contractor established a patch to correct this error and the senior technician received the credit for identifying the problem. He received an award for his efforts. I received a smile of thanks.

Another obstacle occurred when the senior technician that I assisted for years, was about to retire from the Agency. Because we had worked together for so many years, most assumed that his position would be transferred to me immediately, by *right*. There is no such thing as '*by right*' within the agency.

I had been at the facility for almost ten years and there had never been an interview panel for any position held at this particular location. Well, there was a new interview panel process established, effective immediately. When I asked the question, "Why have you just decided to establish interview panels for positions?" The response that I received was that, "We had to start at some time, didn't we?" There were only two applicants for the senior technicians vacated position– myself and another male. When I realized that there was to be a panel, I respectfully declined my application to the position in question. Immediately, the facility decided that there would be no interviews performed for the job. The male applicant automatically received the position. I took that opportunity to apply to transfer to another facility within the Agency, and got the job. At the new facility, things went from bad to worse. As soon as I arrived on site, the bigotry began.

For some reason and I suspect that it was because of my name, the facility management and union representative did not know that I was a Black female. But as soon as that saw me, reality set in for them. At this new facility, I was the only other Black to be selected for a position in air traffic maintenance. The other person was male and management and union was not having that. The first thing that happened was that the union representative for the facility made it his responsibility to ensure that I met prejudice at every turn. He first stated that I needed to temporarily relocate to another facility to learn my job. I was the only one to be forced to that location. The facility manager agreed with him and I was transferred for six months, to another location.

The union representative continued with other petty things. Unfortunately for me, the Union Representative had the backing of my newest Facility Manager. And, the facility manager was the worse.

After spending time at the temporary facility, a new position became available at the other location. So, I applied and , through default, gained the newest position of assistant supervisor. Eventually, I found out that the manager was forced to accept me as the assistant supervisor because of the Affirmative Action processes within the Agency. I represented two minority groups, female and Black. It was a 'Win-Win' for the Facility and a disaster for me. The discriminatory actions took on a whole new life, and everything went downhill from there because everything that I would do, would be reported to the manager.

Several of the employees that were assigned to me, did not follow my supervision. They rebelled at every opportunity. But, it was not everyone. Those who demonstrated racism towards me were few, but they were highly favored by the Management. As a matter of fact, I was informed more times than not that they took their direction from the facility manager and not from me.

I was expected to fail, but I did not. Even with the insubordination, I was able to prepare my assigned unit for upcoming activities. We were ready for every eventuality, and when the newest facility within the FAA was commissioned into the National Airspace (NAS), the group I supervised received high marks for their contribution to the facility's smooth transition, into the NAS. Prior to the facility's commissioning, everyone acknowledged their doubts of me being able to prepare my unit for the new facility opening. My unit was a successful. But because of my efforts of not failing, my direct-report manager gave me a 3, on a scale of 1 to 10, on my performance review. There was to be no award or recognition for a job well done. My immediate supervisor received the accolades, instead.

Because of the successfully, smooth transition into the NAS, the entire facility was authorized to award key players in the transition. But, when I attempted to provide superior performance awards to some of the specialists that were a part of my group, my paperwork was denied by the facility manager. Not only was the paperwork denied approval by the Facility

Manager, but he informed my immediate group's union representative that I did not submit any applications for awards.

I was approached by the union representative and asked why no one received any recognition. He informed me of his conversation with the Manager. I could not verbally defend myself. What was the point. I had already been marked by birth. But I was able to show my email correspondence indicating the rejection from the Manager, and why. The union representative took my word after that incident. You see, I had nothing but my integrity to fight with, and it was good enough for my group's union representative. But there was little that I could do to change the problem of discrimination against me, by those who held the power.

The newer FAA facility was located in an isolated area in the District of Columbia, metro. Because of the isolation, I suggested to the facility manager the possibility of getting automated electronic defibrillators (AED) units at the facility. No other facility within the FAA contained these units, but I felt we had a definite need. My reasoning was that, because of the location and the time it would take for emergency assistance to arrive, time for action may be critical. The AED would be a 'first responder' tool for heart issues.

The Facility Manager stated that he would investigate and get back with me. Months later, I asked about the status of the AED units and was informed by the Manager that the flight surgeon denied the request for establish the units at the facility. One year later, AED units were located throughout the Agency, including our facility.

During my stay at this facility, I was subjected to multiple episodes of hidden racism. I had finally had enough, so I filed an EEO complaint with Civil Rights. Unfortunately, the complaint was returned to me with a statement indicating that I had not filed my complaint through the proper channels.????

Even though the complaint was returned to me, I had had a discussion with my facility manager about his treatment of me. I was in tears. As he sat in my office looking smug, I unloaded. I refused to sit during our discussion. As I stood over my manager, I informed him, in no uncertain terms that, he should not take my tears as a sign of weakness. My back was against the wall and I had no other place to go. For some reason, he finally realized that I meant business and he changed his way of treating me after that conversation. Life went on.

Along came another Sector Manager. He would manager the entire district, but he was even worse than any of the previous managers, combined. His main objective was very clear – eliminate all females within the district. And he was systematically effective. That is, until he went after me. This particular Sector Manager was allowed to say and do whatever he needed to do to accomplish the mission with the full support of the FAA. And his word was final. He was sharp of tongue and slow of wit; his knowledge and understanding of what it took to run a facility was suspect and questionable. Yet, his word was law. After he went eliminated several women from their positions, it was my turn. For a couple of weeks, he would send me emails criticizing my work area and what I was not doing. They started off weekly, then every other day. The emails were petty. Most made no sense. As I checked other facilities, I found that I was the only one receiving these harassing emails. Finally, I had had enough. I filed an Accountability Board complaint based on Racial Discrimination. Two days later, my complaint was reject via a voicemail response stating that, "because my complaint was based on Racial Discrimination, it was not an Accountability Board issue and the case was close."??? At that time, the Accountability Board would not investigate any matter other than the seven that they identified with. All others were not their issue, and they provided no direction on how to handle other matters. I immediately filed an EEO complaint and immediately, the email harassment trailed stopped.

But the EEO complaint process was a farce. Within the government, unless you have the resources to gain a powerful attorney, you will fail. They expect this to happen for most cases and so they wait their time. The Agency's complaint process was designed to exhaust your efforts before you became successful, and very few government employees have $20,000.00 minimum, just to retain an attorney.

So, after over a year of communications back and forth with Civil Rights, and two mediation later, I received a response on my EEO complaint, stating that I did not file my paperwork, in a timely manner. As far as the Agency was concerned, my complaint was closed and final.

Another incident happened when I filed a memo with my manager, requesting that he investigate and reprimand a person for information leaks and insubordination. After no activity on my complaint, I, along with another supervisor, were called into the manager's office to discuss my memo. Immediately, I was informed that he would not discipline this person because we had

not mentored the employee. The employee was
a junior employee and it was our fault that this
happened. We were verbally reprimanded for
dereliction of duty. Did I mention that she did not
report to either one of us; she reported directly to
the manager. Eventually, the Sector manager
got promoted, and I got labelled throughout the
FAA.

My husband transferred to another location and I
attempted to transfer there, also. Though I made
many attempts, I was only successful in gaining a
position at the new location, with a downgrade
in pay. I also had to pay for my own transfer. I
was curious as to why I was unable to gain
employment in positions similar to the one that I
was working in. When I request debriefs from the
other positions that I applied for, I was informed
that I did not qualify for some of the positions that
I applied for or I was overqualified, and the
others just didn't respond at all. I guess they felt
that they didn't need to respond. One did
respond to me indicating that they wanted
someone with no experience in supervision, as
the supervisor.

When I finally re-located to the next location and
the lower-grade position, the bigotry and bias
continued. My newest position was a riot of
prejudices.

I was happy to be doing a job that was completely different from supervising people. Being a frontline supervisor is a 'thankless' position in any agency, but in air traffic maintenance, it was the most difficult. But in my newest position as a training specialist, you have no rights whatsoever, and I found out the hard way.

I was content in my new position but not its location. The drive to the location was 'suicide by traffic' and isolated. Some days I felt uncomfortable about going into the unsecured location, so I thought that I would attempt to work at a detached site location. When I asked my manager if this would be possible, he immediately informed me that, "No, I could not work at the other location because there were employees who had been there longer than me who may want to work there." I thought that that was a legitimate response until a few weeks later, a new employee was given the opportunity to work at the other location because she lived in that area. I was senior to her but she was not Black.

Another incident I was subjected to involved a very staunch Republican and racist, ex-air traffic controller. Due to some prior incident with the agency, she was given an administrative desk position but she was able to maintain her air traffic pay. Because she was still considered an air traffic controller, she felt it her job to 'rule' over the technical operations personnel at this site. After being subjected to her efforts of condescension, we had a verbal discussion. When I informed my supervisor of the harassment, she informed me that "It was not my position to say anything to the other employee and it was not her (my supervisor) position to deal with the matter." There would be no help from that area.

Because of my technical background, I offered to assist with the maintenance of the telephone switch located at the facility. The person that my supervisor assigned refused to work with the equipment because he stated that it was not his job. I enjoyed doing that type of work, and it gave me something to do on my slow days.

The ex-air traffic controller approached me, in reprimand for assigning a telephone to another employee. This was a part of the work that I was assisting the facility with. I did not report to her, and informed her of this. When I talked with my supervisor about her interference, she reprimanded me for talking back to the administrative clerk in a negative manner. I informed my manager that I would be relinquishing my work with the voice switch because it would involve direct contact with the ex-air traffic controller. I was given a negative review because of it. The employee who refused to do the work because it was not his job, received an award and a pay raise.

This type of pettiness went on for three years. Finally, I got another position out of there, even though I had not recently applied for it.   I received an offer of temporary employee on the same day that I got my last negative review. My supervisor informed me, that because I did not write my own review and she knew nothing of what I was doing in my position, she would give me, a barely passing, review. It was time to leave.

In the newest position, I eventually found out the manager did not want the person who scored the highest points to receive the position, and that is how I got the job. Again, by default. Later, I found out that that person was a Black Male.

At the newest location, fresh new faces continued with the same old racism. My unit's union representative attempted to intimidate me. It was not effective. My performance of the tasks assigned to me, was always questioned. I could never succeed at my efforts. I was criticized for issues that others received praise for.

Awards were few and positive recognition was – never. The only thing that got me through the last of my positions within the Agency was the people who I had supervisory oversight for. The saying that, "people can make or break you", is exactly how I felt about the specialists who worked within the units that I supervised. Without their efforts, I would not have been able to make it through most of the trying times within the Agency. There are a lot of great and talented people within the FAA who continues to do what needs to be done. I can say that I worked with many of them, and appreciate their presence in my life. But there are enough racial and gender bigots still employed within the Government, that will continue the work of the other bigots of the past. Unfortunately, there are also employees of the Black race, that will ensure that the bigots succeed in their efforts.

Eventually, I retired from the Agency. I had had enough of the bigotry and hidden racism. It was affecting my ability to perform my job, and that was what their efforts were attempting to do. I could not let them succeed.

One of the things that I did learned throughout the entire process, is that the Federal Government is the biggest perpetrators of discrimination. Because of this, the few employees who perform such acts, have no problem continuing in their efforts to commit acts of bigotry towards their fellow employees. Why would anyone be concerned about disciplinary actions when you already know how easy it is to get away with your discriminatory practices. From my perspective, the FAA systematically demonstrates hidden racism at every opportunity. And why would it change now that the 'perfect storm' is brewing in the White House? The strongest support for acts of discrimination within the government, is alive and well today and can be found at the highest level of government. Discriminatory practices within, or outside of the Government, will not improve because we will not change our complacency. The entire governmental climate is rancid with the foul odor and decay of discrimination.

As of this writing, there has not been a Black American to hold the highest position of administrator, within the FAA. There have been individuals from all other races and gender, but not one Black. I doubt that this pattern of discrimination will change within my lifetime.

Were all of my negative experiences within the government, the 'Hell' of my own making? If they were, why are there so many EEO and Accountability Board complaints filed other Black employees, within the government. Are they all frivolous or legitimate complaints? You decide. But if you believe that most are frivolous, just remember the years of presidency from 2008 to 2016. Can you truly state that any one president prior to the 2008 presidency, experienced so many negative issues? Did any president prior to 2008, experience such scrutiny on everything that they did, on every decision that they made, on every word that was said, to the point that any efforts that were made for the people of the U.S. were purposely shot down, just because the concept was developed during the term of office of a Black President? If you believe that the government does not perpetrate racial discrimination against Black people, then you can never see past what reality is. You will remain clueless. At some point, I believe that we all have been clueless. The President, during the 2008 - 2016 term of office, probably never thought that such a level of hatred and bigotry existed until he too, experienced it, firsthand.

No matter how many racial ethnicities there are, or how high a percentage that each may represent in a person's DNA, in this society of racial hatred, your Black count overrules.   It will not matter how little sub-Saharan blood that you may contain and how high the levels are for other races, you will still be considered Black when the dust settles. Check the laws on the books if you don't believe it.

CHAPTER 3
Urban Blight

As Black America struggles to survive in the 'world of man', we are constantly running into new obstacles along the way. Do we recognize them as obstacles or do we ignore the obvious and worry about our own little world? Personally, I can say that ignoring the obvious has been a way of life. But as I get older, I realize that that is the worst thing that Black Americans, as a race, can do to themselves.

As Black Americans prosper, we do not recognize that our own identities our disappearing. We went from being identified as 'Colored', to 'Negro', to Afro-American, to 'Black American', and now African American. African American is a very strong moniker, but it does not individualize our race. Are there not many different races in Africa? If a person born and raised in Africa and re-locates to American, regardless of their race, are they not also considered African American? When we lose our identity, what's next? Our security, as well?

Our neighborhoods are suffering, our education is suffering, and our financial stability is suffering. Yet, we do not recognize it for what it is – another form of slavery.

Throughout history, race riots directed at Blacks, have been successful in one main area – the minimalization and/or total destruction of Black dominant growth and prosperity, in any community.

If you revisit history, there have been many race riots involving Blacks. The one thing that stood out for these riots is the destabilization of an entire race of people. Four of the most devastating race riots – 1898 Wilmington, NC[1]; 1906 Atlanta, GA[2]; 1921 Tulsa, OK[3]; 1923 Rosewood, FL[4] – saw the mass destruction of prominent and influential Blacks, and their properties.

1898 Wilmington, NC [1]In 1898, Wilmington was a thriving port city on the coast of North Carolina. About two-thirds of Wilmington's population was African American. African Americans were business people who owned barbershops, restaurants, tailor shops, and drug stores. African Americans also held positions as firemen and policemen. Overall, the African American and white races existed peacefully but separately.

Good relations continued until the election of 1896, when the white Democrats lost control of state politics. A group of predominately white Populists and African American Republicans won political control of the state. The white Democrats promised to avenge their defeat at the hands of white Populists and African American Republicans in the election of 1898. Daniel Schenck, a Democratic party leader, warned, "It will be the meanest, vilest, dirtiest campaign since 1876" (the election that ended reconstruction in the South).

The Democratic campaign focused on white women's fears of African American males and the threat of African American men being lynched. Prior to the election, a white newspaper in Wilmington published a controversial speech

34

given by a Georgia feminist. In her speech she supported the lynching of African American males for inappropriate relationships with white women. Alex Manly, an African American newspaper editor in Wilmington, was infuriated by the newspaper article. Mr. Manly wrote editorials in his newspaper arguing that white males were just as guilty of having inappropriate relationships with African American women. Exchange of words between the two newspapers increased racial tensions. Alfred Moore Waddell, a former Confederate officer and U.S. Congressman, called for the removal of the Republicans and Populists then in power in Wilmington. He proposed in a speech that the white citizens, if necessary, should "choke the Cape Fear with carcasses."

African American voters turned out in large numbers for the election of 1898. However, the Democrats who favored white supremacy stuffed the ballot boxes and won the election. Two days after the election, violence erupted into the "Wilmington Race Riot." About 500 white men had assembled at the armory, and Waddell lead them to the Daily Record office several blocks away. The crowd following Waddell grew to about 2,000 people as they moved across town.

During what is now called the Wilmington Race Riot, a mob set Alex Manly's newspaper office on fire, and tensions between African Americans and whites exploded. Whites demanded that Manly and his newspaper cease to publish and that Manly be banned from the community. Manly escaped from Wilmington because he was mistakenly thought to be white. African Americans armed themselves and whites began to hunt and gun them down. The mob of whites included clergymen, lawyers, bankers, and merchants who all believed that they were asserting their rights as citizens. When the riot ended the next day, it was reported that twenty-five African Americans had been killed. However, it was strongly suspected that hundreds of African Americans had been killed and their bodies dumped into the river. In addition, hundreds of African

Americans were banished from the city of Wilmington. This event, the Wilmington Race Riot, marked a turning point in North Carolina's history because more restrictions were placed on African American voters.

[1] *(information provided by North Carolina Freedom Movement Project to LEARNNC.ORG)*

1906 Atlanta, GA[2] 1880s Atlanta had become the hub of the regional economy, and the city's overall population soared from 89,000 in 1900 to 150,000 in 1910; the black population was approximately 9,000 in 1880 and 35,000 by 1900. Such growth put pressure on municipal services, increased job competition among black and white workers, heightened class distinctions, and led the city's white leadership to respond with restrictions intended to control the daily behavior of the growing working class, with mixed success. Such conditions caused concern among elite whites, who feared the social intermingling of the races, and led to an expansion of Jim Crow segregation, particularly in the separation of white and black neighborhoods and separate seating areas for public transportation.
The emergence during this time of a black elite in Atlanta also contributed to racial tensions in the city.

During Reconstruction (1867-76), black men were given the right to vote, and as blacks became more involved in the political realm, they began to establish business, create social networks, and build communities. As this black elite acquired wealth, education, and prestige, its members attempted to distance themselves from an affiliation with the black working class, and especially from the unemployed black men who frequented the saloons on Atlanta's Decatur Street. Many whites, while uncomfortable with the advances of the black elite, also disapproved of these saloons, which were said to be decorated with depictions of nude women. Concern over such establishments fueled prohibition advocates in the city, and many whites began to blame black saloon-goers for rising crime rates in the growing city, and particularly for threats of black sexual violence against white women.

The candidates for the 1906 governor's race played to white fears of a black upper class. In the months leading up to the August election, both Hoke Smith, the former publisher of the *Atlanta Journal*, and Clark Howell, the editor of the *Atlanta Constitution*, were in the position as gubernatorial candidates to influence public opinion through their newspapers. Smith, with the public support of former Populist Thomas E. Watson, inflamed racial tensions in Atlanta by insisting that black disenfranchisement was necessary to ensure that blacks were kept "in their place"; that is, in a position inferior to that of whites. Since receiving the right to vote, Smith argued, blacks also had sought economic and social equality. By disenfranchising blacks, whites could maintain the social order. Howell, on the other hand, claimed that the Democratic white primary and the poll tax were already sufficient in limiting black voting. Instead, Howell emphasized that Smith was not the racial separatist he claimed to be, and he charged that Smith had in the past cooperated with black political leaders and thus could not be relied upon to advance the cause of white supremacy.

In addition to the political debates waged in the *Journal* and the *Constitution*, other newspapers, especially the *Atlanta Georgian* and the *Atlanta News*, carried stories throughout the year about alleged assaults on white women by black men. The media provoked anger and hatred in its white readers—with stories, editorials, and cartoons warning of rising crime, the danger to white women of rape by black males, the disreputable saloons that encouraged drunkenness and licentious behavior in "brutish" men, and the desire of "uppity" blacks to achieve equality with whites. By late September, after newspaper reports of four separate incidences of alleged assaults by blacks on white women circulated in Atlanta, mob violence erupted.

Chapter 3

The Riot

On the afternoon of Saturday, September 22, Atlanta newspapers reported four alleged assaults, none of which were ever substantiated, upon local white women. Extra editions of these accounts, sensationalized with lurid details and inflammatory language intended to inspire fear if not revenge, circulated, and soon thousands of white men and boys gathered in downtown Atlanta. City leaders, including Mayor James G. Woodward, sought to calm the increasingly indignant crowds but failed to do so. By early evening, the crowd had become a mob; from then until after midnight, they surged down Decatur Street, Pryor Street, Central Avenue, and throughout the central business district, assaulting hundreds of blacks. The mob attacked black-owned businesses, smashing the windows of black leader Alonzo Herndon's barbershop. Although Herndon had closed down early and was already at home when his shop was damaged, another barbershop across the street was raided by the rioters—and the barbers were killed. The crowd also attacked streetcars, entering trolley cars and beating black men and women; at least three men were beaten to death.

Finally, the militia was summoned around midnight, and streetcar service was suspended. The mob showed no signs of letting up, however, and the crowd was dispersed only once a heavy rain began to fall around 2:00 a.m. Atlanta was then under the control of the state militia.

On Sunday, September 23, the Atlanta newspapers reported that the state militia had been mustered to control the mob; they also reported that blacks were no longer a problem for whites because Saturday night's violence had driven them off public streets. While the police, armed with rifles, and militia patrolled the streets and key landmarks and guarded white property, blacks secretly obtained weapons to arm themselves against the mob, fearing its return. Despite the presence of law enforcement, white vigilante groups invaded some black neighborhoods. In some areas African Americans defended their homes and were able to turn away the incursions into their communities. (One person who described such activity was Walter White, who experienced the riot as a young boy. The incident was a defining moment for White, who went on to become secretary of the National Association for the Advancement of Colored People [NAACP], and he later described the event in his 1948 memoir *A Man Called White*.)

On Monday, September 24, a group of African Americans held a meeting in Brownsville, a community located about two miles south of downtown Atlanta and home to the historically black Clark College (later Clark Atlanta University) and Gammon Theological Seminary. The blacks were heavily armed. When Fulton County police learned of the gathering, they feared a counterattack and launched a raid on Brownsville. A shootout ensued, and an officer was killed. In response, three companies of heavily armed militia were sent to Brownsville, where they seized weapons and arrested more than 250 African American men. Meanwhile, sporadic fighting continued throughout the day.

Aftermath

On Monday and Tuesday, city officials, businessmen, clergy, and the press called for an end to violence, because it was damaging Atlanta's image as a thriving New South city. Indeed, the riot had been covered throughout the United States as well as internationally. Fears of continued disorder prompted some white civic leaders to seek a dialogue with black elites, establishing a rare biracial tradition that convinced mainstream northern whites that racial reconciliation was possible in the South without national intervention. Paired with black fears of renewed violence, however, this interracial cooperation exacerbated black social divisions as the black elite sought to distance itself from the lower class and its interests, leaving the city among the most segregated and socially stratified in the nation.

Newspaper accounts at the time and subsequent scholarly treatments of the riot vary widely on the number of casualties. Estimates range from twenty-five to forty African American deaths, although the city coroner issued only ten death certificates for black victims. Most accounts agree that only two whites were killed, one of whom was a woman who suffered a heart attack on seeing the mob outside her home.

There were other consequences of the riot as well, both locally and nationally. Its aftermath saw a depression of Atlanta's black community and economy. The riot contributed to the passage of statewide prohibition and black suffrage restriction by 1908. It discredited for many black leaders the accommodationist strategy of Booker T. Washington among the leadership of black America, and gave new legitimacy to the more aggressive tactics for achieving racial justice epitomized by W. E. B. Du Bois, who wrote a powerful poem, "The Litany of Atlanta," in the riot's wake. Although it had a profound effect on many of those who experienced it, the riot was forgotten or minimized for decades in the white community and ignored in official histories of the city.

[2] *Information provided by*
http://www.georgiaencyclopedia.org/articles/history-archaeology/atlanta-race-riot-1906

1921 Tulsa, OK[3] In 1921, Tulsa had the wealthiest black neighborhood in the country. On Sundays, women wore satin dresses and diamonds, while men wore silk shirts and gold chains. In Greenwood, writes historian James S. Hirsch, "Teachers lived in brick homes furnished with Louis XIV dining room sets, fine china, and Steinway pianos."

They called it Black Wall Street.

"They had done everything that they were supposed to do in terms of the American dream," says Carol Anderson, Professor of African American Studies at Emory University. "You work hard, you save your money, you go to school, you buy property. And this is what they had done under horrific conditions."

Greenwood was strictly segregated from the rest of the city, but still it flourished. It was home to black lawyers, business owners, and doctors—including Dr. A.C. Jackson, who was considered the most skilled black surgeon in America and had a net worth of $100,000.

Dr. Jackson was killed on the night of May 31st, 1921, along with hundreds of black Tulsans. Thirty-five blocks of Greenwood were razed that night. 1,256 homes and 191 businesses were destroyed. 10,000 black people were left homeless. By morning, Black Wall Street had been reduced to rubble.

The story begins: In 1890, a group of migrants fleeing the hostile South settled an all-black town called Langston, 80 miles west of Tulsa. Oklahoma wasn't yet a state, and its racial dynamics weren't set in stone. The architect of the settlement, Edwin McCabe, had a vision of Oklahoma as the black promised land. He sent recruiters to the South, preaching racial pride and self-sufficiency. At least 29 black separatist towns were established in Oklahoma during the late 19th century.

White homesteaders opposed to the "Africanization of Oklahoma" spearheaded a counter-movement, and the rural black settlements were all but wiped off the map. McCabe himself fled to Chicago in 1908. But black people were in Oklahoma for good, and they moved to the cities—taking that dream of empowerment with them.

41

Tulsa experienced a massive oil boom in the 1900s, and black residents began making good money as cooks and domestic servants to the freewheeling white *nouveau riche*. They invested that money in their own neighborhood, and by 1920 Greenwood was the most vibrant and affluent black community in the United States.

White residents were disturbed by the growing black wealth in Greenwood, and sought to impose official segregation measures. In 1914, the city passed a law that forbade anyone from living on a block where more than three quarters of the preexisting residents were of another race. In isolation, Greenwood only thrived more. Its main strip boasted attorneys' offices, auto shops, cafes, a movie theater, funeral homes, pool halls, beauty salons, grocery stores, furriers and confectioneries.

One entrepreneur built an elegant 54-room hotel, likely the largest ever owned by a black person in pre-Civil Rights America. Crystal chandeliers hung from the ceiling in the banquet hall. Its owner, J.B. Stradford, had been born a slave.

"That resentment in Tulsa was so intense," says Carol Anderson, "it was just waiting for a spark in order to ignite it." That spark was a sexual assault allegation against a black teenager named Dick Rowland. It's not entirely clear what happened in the elevator of the Drexel Building on May 30, 1921, but one common narrative is that Rowland accidentally tripped against its operator, a white 17-year-old named Sarah Page, causing her to scream.

A bystander who heard the scream called the police, and "like a game of telephone, the story became more inflammatory with each retelling, and spread rapidly," writes Dexter Mullins.

When Rowland was captured, a few black World War I veterans from Greenwood armed themselves in front of the courthouse, prepared to prevent a lynching. They were justified in their fear—a man named Roy Belton had been lynched in Tulsa the year before, after his arrest. "The lynching of Roy Belton," read Greenwood's black newspaper *The Tulsa Star* in 1920, "explodes the theory that a prisoner is safe on the top of the Court House from mob violence."

In front of the courthouse where Dick Rowland was being kept, a group of white men approached the black men from Greenwood. "Nigger, what are you going to do with that pistol?" said one.

"I'm going to use it if I need to," the black man replied.

The white man attempted to wrest the pistol from his hands, and a gunshot rang out. It's unclear whether it was accidental, a warning shot, or an attempt to injure or kill. In any case, all hell broke loose.

The groups of white and black men had a running gunfight all the way to Greenwood. When they got there, the group of whites—which had grown in number—began firing indiscriminately on black bystanders. Black people were shot in the streets, and dragged behind cars with nooses tied around their necks. Their houses and businesses were looted and burned down. Greenwood residents fired back, and there were white casualties as well. Ultimately, the white mob was larger and better armed.

Many eyewitness accounts mention planes flying overhead. One, written by the black lawyer Buck Colbert Franklin, reads: "Smoke ascended the sky in thick, black volumes and amid it all, the planes—now a dozen or more in number—still hummed and darted here and there with the agility of natural birds of the air… The sidewalks were literally covered with burning turpentine balls."

An official report published by the city in 2001 confirmed that some of the planes were flown by police conducting reconnaissance. The others, it concluded, were probably piloted by white civilians who fired ammunition and dropped bottles of gasoline on the buildings below.

In the middle of the night, the Tulsa police formally requested that the National Guard assist them in quelling what they called a "Negro uprising." As they awaited the National Guard, they let Greenwood burn.

When the soldiers arrived, they detained 6,000 black residents, many of them for more than a week. Upon release, these residents were homeless. In 2016 numbers, more than $30 million worth of property damage was sustained.

"Tulsa civic leaders clung to conservative estimates," writes historian Tim Madigan, but "the number of the dead no doubt climbed well into the hundreds, making the burning in Tulsa the deadliest domestic American outbreak since the Civil War."

The Ku Klux Klan's presence in Tulsa was bolstered in the years following the massacre. But while the KKK remains active, the resistance of black Tulsans has survived too: a 1996 rally was interrupted when Tiffaeny Lanigan confronted Klan members with a lone raised fist.

After the massacre, Greenwood was uninhabitable. Former residents lived in Red Cross tents for months, through the freezing winter.

The Tulsa Real Estate Exchange attempted to make it prohibitively expensive to rebuild Greenwood. A founder of Tulsa named W. Tate Brady—also a Klansman—had taken control of the Exchange, and devised a plan to relocate black residents even further away from the city center. The Exchange prepared building codes to make the area industrial instead of residential.

But even with everything in ruins, former Greenwood residents fought back. Buck Colbert Franklin took the case to the Oklahoma Supreme Court, which declared the city's efforts to forestall redevelopment unconstitutional.

Tulsa's black population set about rebuilding, and it held on for a few more decades. But Greenwood was never the same. In the 1970s, much of it was leveled to make room for a highway.

The official investigation in 2001 found the city partly responsible for the casualties and property damage of the Tulsa massacre. In its section "Assessing State and City Culpability," the report mentions not only the passivity of police, but their active involvement in the mob violence. It reads, "Tulsa failed to take action to protect against the riot. More important, city officials deputized men right after the riot broke out. Some of those deputies—probably in conjunction with some uniformed police officers—were responsible for some of the burning of Greenwood."

Otis Clarke, a survivor of the 1921 Tulsa massacre, filed a brief in 2005 at the U.S. Supreme Court in Washington. on behalf of the remaining victims.

The report concluded that the City of Tulsa owed reparations to the survivors of the massacre and their descendants. Those reparations have yet to be paid.

The survivors of the Tulsa Race Massacre are nearly all dead now. And the mob violence they endured not only traumatized them as individuals—it destroyed black wealth in Tulsa, and set the parameters for race relations in the city for the next century.

"Black success was an intolerable affront to the social order of white supremacy," writes Hirsch, "so taking their possessions not only stripped Blacks of their material status, but also tipped the social scales back to their proper alignment." In Tulsa today, as elsewhere, that alignment remains strikingly unequal.

[3] *Information provided via https://timelinecom/history-tulsa-race-massacre, as presented by Meagan Day*

1923 Rosewood, FL[4]

Rosewood: The Last Survivor Remembers an American Tragedy

Historian Dr. Marvin Dunn interviews the last survivor of Rosewood and sheds new light on the event that still haunts African-Americans.

She was the last person alive with a living memory of Rosewood the north Florida black town that was consumed in racial rage this week more than eight decades ago. She was eight when it happened and her memory was as clear as a bell. Robie Mortin and Historian Dr. Marvin Dunn were friends. They met when Mortin was well into her nineties living in an assisted living complex in West Palm Beach where what was left of her family settled after the event.

"I was in third grade," she once told me. "I could read and write. I remember everything;" like playing in her aunt Sarah Carrier's yard every Sunday after church, like the plum trees that grew in her yard, like getting apples at Christmas and dancing and playing games on Emancipation Day; and the night the mob burned the town down.

Rosewood had been the perfect storm for racial violence. All of the usual suspects applied, an alleged sexual attack by a black man on a white woman, a black man with an attitude and lots of friends who had guns, economic jealousy because many blacks in Rosewood were doing better than the back woods whites who lived around them and the killing by blacks of a white law enforcement officer.

It had all been a lie. Mortin had heard the stories over the years. The white woman, Fannie Taylor was having an affair and almost got caught when her lover beat her one morning while her husband was at work. Fannie said a black man did it and that was all it took. Over the following week hundreds of white men descended upon Rosewood vengeance in mind and torches in hand. Sylvester Carrier would emerge as the hero of the moment. He gathered up his family and hunkered down in his mother's large two-story home. He was a Mason.

"Almost all of the men out there were Masons", Mortin recalled. The night the mob came to the Carrier House an unknown number of heavily armed black men were waiting. Some were hidden in the woods. It was a gathering of Masons. When it was all over eight people were dead including Sylvester and his mother Sarah, Robie's aunt.
4Above excerpt from thegrio, dated January 4, 2012, as reported by Historian Dr. Marvin Dunn

A similar report of the race riot of Rosewood is as follows:

On January 1, 1923 a massacre was carried out in the small, predominantly black town of Rosewood in Central Florida. The massacre was instigated by the rumor that a white woman, Fanny Taylor, had been sexually assaulted by a black man in her home in a nearby community. A group of white men, believing this rapist to be a recently escaped convict named Jesse Hunter who was hiding in Rosewood, assembled to capture this man.

Prior this event a series of incidents had stirred racial tensions within Rosewood. During the previous winter of 1922 a white school teacher from Perry had been murdered and on New Year's Eve of 1922 there was a Ku Klux Klan rally held in Gainesville, located not far away from Rosewood.

In response to the allegation by Taylor, white men began to search for Jesse Hunter, Aaron Carrier and Sam Carter who were believed to be accomplices. Carrier was captured and incarcerated while Carter was lynched. The white mob suspected Aaron's cousin, Sylvester Carrier, a Rosewood resident of harboring the fugitive, Jesse Hunter.

On January 4, 1923 a group of 20 to 30 white men approached the Carrier home and shot the family dog. When Sylvester's mother Sarah came to the porch to confront the mob they shot and killed her. Sylvester defended his home, killing two men and wounding four in the ensuing battle before he too was killed. The remaining survivors fled to the swamps for refuge where many of the African American residents of Rosewood had already retreated, hoping to avoid the rising conflict and increasing racial tension.

The next day the white mob burned the Carrier home before joining with a group of 200 men from surrounding towns who had heard erroneously that a black man had killed two white men. As night descended the mob attacked the town, slaughtering animals and burning buildings. An official report claims six blacks killed along with two whites. Other accounts suggest a larger total. At the end of the carnage only two buildings remained standing, a house and the town general store.

Many of the black residents of Rosewood who fled to the swamps were evacuated on January 6 by two local train conductors, John and William Bryce. Many others were hidden by John Wright, the owner of the general store. Other black residents of Rosewood fled to Gainesville and to northern cities. As a consequence of the massacre, Rosewood became deserted.

[4] *Information provided through* http://www.blackpast.org/aah/rosewood-massacre-1923

Throughout history, this type of racial injustice continued to take place, with very little if any, consequences to the perpetrators.

Although it is impossible to physically 'burn out' an entire community of people today because of the laws, without being held accountable, there are other ways to effectively 'burn out' an entire race of people so that the establishment of prominence and dominance does not exist for any large community of Blacks.

When the country went from systemic segregation to partial integration, blacks were immediately bused from their comfort zones. All of a sudden, gone was the level of quality education that fostered the powerful minds of Blacks of the pre-Civil rights movement. Now, in order to get the type of education of that era,

Chapter 3

you have to pay for it, and very few Blacks have the financial ability to do so. The system is designed that we should be able to politically-vote for improvements and change, yet we do not, and our children - our future, suffers.

I remember the type of education that I received prior to integration. The teachers were dedicated and hard taskmasters, yet their goals were simple - to ensure that we had the foundation to succeed.

I remember my first school outside of the black community, when schools were integrated. The teachers were not happy to teach us and the extra-curricular athletic activities were curtailed. That same school went so far as to drain the school's pool, so that no blacks would be able to swim in it. It was routinely demonstrated to us that, although national mandate dictated that all schools would be integrated, all students did not have to be educated. This effectively demonstrated that there is always a way around the law, and a creative mind can find that loophole. If you look closely at your school systems today, you can easily see that 'hidden racism' exists. Though you pay taxes like everyone else, are those taxes used in your neighborhoods, or are they used more prevalently in the more affluent, and less colorful areas of the population?

Another form of 'hidden racism' is urban blight. Remember when the District of Columbia use to be called 'Chocolate City? Well, not anymore. And Detroit was strong in black influence and culture. The popularity of many cities with strong black culture, wealth, education, and economic growth eventually suffer from a decline in infrastructure support from the government, and yet we do nothing to stop the decline. Poverty becomes the norm and crime is on the rise. Instead of staying and fighting the problem, we run. As a matter of fact, we buy into the reported reasons for the decline, and we move to the suburbs.

Have you ever taken notice that many of the prominent cities in the U.S., that had been racially-diverse, with a strong Black presence, eventually suffer from job losses and abject poverty? Once the Black population numbers have dwindled from the metropolis; that particular metropolitan area experiences a sudden 'renaissance' of economic infusion and infrastructure improvements that we, as Black Americans, are not a part of. WHY???

In the past, we were burned out, but now we are economically-starved out. There is a large difference between the two processes, but the results are still the same. Blacks have been effectively eliminated, and the area is now available for revitalization. And we have very little involvement in the regrowth.

 Black America has literally taken the bait - hook, line and sinker. When will we learn the game? Or do we want to learn the game? The average person, of any race, do not think so nefariously that he or she believe that this type of activity goes on in our communities. The reality, is that it does.

As a race of people, Blacks need to wake up and realize that with all of the senseless killings of our youth, the pedaling of flesh of our young, and the infusion of drugs to our people, we will continue to be enslaved to the system. Not by the hands of others but by our own hands, and we will have no one to blame but ourselves. Wake up people and do the right thing for yourself and your communities. Be the change, that will make the change to improve your own little corner of the world. We are a powerful race of people who have contributed greatly to the establishment of the youngest, yet most powerful country in the world. Take some ownership in it.

CHAPTER 4

We Just Want to be Left to Live

The average non-Black American probably feels the same as the average Black American. We just want to be left alone to live our lives and enjoy the fruits of our labor. Black America is just like White America – we go to work and pay bills; we pay taxes and wait for our refunds; we seek out good education and we pay for higher learning; we spend time with our family and friends; we invest and we grow; we educate and are educated; we mow our lawns and harvest our fields; we work to live and live to enjoy life. We are only human, and no different than anyone else. We want the same things that others want, and we work hard to get those things and maintain them.

Back when Europeans decided that it would be best to leave their home country and venture to the new world, their goal was simple – to live a life without stricture; to be considered as equals and to be left alone to live and thrive. Europeans came to the new world with high hopes and dreams, to be able to co-exist and make a future for themselves and their families. They came to a world that was already occupied with a people whose culture was not like their own. The culture of the American Indian was normal to the Indians, but considered 'savage' to the new arrivals. Yet, it was their culture and it worked for the Indians, and it also helped some Europeans adapt to the new world – to survive. Unfortunately, the American Indians' world was about to take on a metamorphic change that would mark the beginning of the end of their world as they knew it.

It's the End of the World, As We Know It

Who knew the enormity of changes that would occur because a couple of ships ran off course, so many centuries ago. I suspect that if the Indians knew then what they know now, they would have kept their knowledge of survival to themselves. But, as with any race, it is just human nature to want to help others, not hurt them.   But hurt does happen even under the best intentions. It is not everyone who purposefully invokes the hurt, but the few who have done this by design, will have followers who will continue to do so in the future. Human nature is human nature, and time will never heal the need for absolute power over others. Even when the majority of the population gets along with each other, some have that feral need to control. The American Indians found that out the hard way, and so did my ancestors.

The Europeans found that surviving in the new world was not going to be easy. Living what the Europeans believed was a harsh life in Great Britain, did not prepare them for the reality of the actual harsh life of a world, untamed. Forgetting about how difficult it was to survive the barbaric plains of Europe, most probably thought that the new world would be a 'piece of cake'. As they soon found out, this was not to be. As, through the ages in Europe, many areas were wild and barbaric, the new world proved to be no less different.

The work was hard and back-breaking, and the ability to sustain life in a world unknown, was a great challenge. In order to survive, they needed help and the Indians were willing to give that help. But the Native Americans would soon learn that they would not know at how high a price.

The work was back-breaking and the newcomers were not able to sustain the workload. The enslaved and the hired Indians, Hispanics, and Asians could not endure the amount of labor needed to build the New World. Nor were they able to support the prosperity of this new race of people entering this World, unknown. But when a deal was made with the devil to, not only capture but enslave another race of people who were sold out by their own kind, the tide finally turned favorably for the New World order.

In order to eliminate the competition in the African motherland, tribes sold off their people to a group of prominent and aggressive Europeans. The people were chained and corralled; treated worse that livestock. They were transported in the hulls of ships where they remained chained until they arrived at the ports for sale. At that point, they would travel again to their final locations. But at their final locations, life could be no better. Not only were the African people kept chained, but families were separated – never to meet again. The treatment was inhuman. Animals were better treated than the average slave. For a slave, starvation and flogging was a daily occurrence; rape and sodomizing was the masters' favorite forms of entertainment; and yet they still survived and thrive. A race of people who knew no comfort, yet they continued to show respect. What does that say about a race of people who have never known peace? That we are survivors, and we are compassionate. We just want to live and be left alone to enjoy the 'fruits of our labor'.

Yet even in 2017, there are those who see that that is too much for a race of people that should have been extinct a long time ago. We are feared for no other reason than the fact that we have survived as a race, and continue to survive and thrive. Will this ever end, or is it our 'lot' in life? My ancestors did not ask to come to the new world, they were dragged here, against their will, **IN CHAINS**. Now that we are here, we are here to stay and for those who feel that we should go back to where we came from, we basically came from here. Black Americans have a unique quality, in that our ancestors were imported as enslaved Black Cargo, but every

Chapter 5

other race's ancestors came freely as
immigrated. Think about why European
ancestors came to the new world in the first
place – to get away from 'class standards'. My
Black African ancestors were dragged here. No
other race of people can make that claim. My
ancestors did not ask to come here, but we, their
descendants, are here to stay.

CHAPTER 6
Racial Inequality

I saw a video of an autopsy once. It was very interesting and eye-opening. The autopsy was of two men who have died in separate incidents. One died in a fire and the other died of unknown reasons. The irony of the autopsy process was that while the medical examiner was attempting to demonstrate the autopsy procedures, I learned something more important. What I learned was that underneath the skin, we are all the same color. Looking at the bodies, there was no immediate way to tell which body was Black or which body was Caucasian, because the subdermal layers where the same color.

With that said, not one person who has ever lived, had the ability to decide what race they would be born to. We have no ability to decide our race, creed, color, nationality, gender, eye shape or color, skin tone or texture, hair texture or color. And if there is anyone who believes that they have control over these factors, it is madness.

That is the beauty of the world we live in, that we are all unique in our own way. To victimize, dehumanize, or demonize a person because of uncontrollable factors of birth, equates to madness.

I have heard too many times, criticisms of a race of people because one got something that the other felt was theirs, by right of birth. If you don't have what you believe that you are supposed to have, work to achieve it.   Stop blaming others for your incompetence. If you don't have what you believe is yours by right, it is because you did not work for it. Don't blame me – blame yourself and fix it.

To all races of people of the World in general, using bigotry and prejudice to hide behind the fact that you have not worked or attempted to work to get what you want is just a typical example of weakness on your part. Don't blame an entire race of people for the dumb and stupid actions of a few. Look at your own race first before you look at others. We are only human, and all races have flaws. I did not take anything from you. All that I have, I have earned due to my own efforts and not off of the backs of others.

Historically, we have contributed substantially to the growth and prosperity of the United States, from the building of this country off the backs of slaves to the continued building and protection of this country voluntarily, through our actions. We are a major factor in the success of this nation and asked to be treated with the respect that we are long overdue. Give us a break and

put your bitterness aside. This country is big
enough for all of us to work and grow together.

CHAPTER 7
Black is Beautiful

The world is full of beautiful people. Every race, across the globe has distinctly beautiful people, and the Black American race is no different.

If you look closely at the Black American race of people, anyone can see that we run the entire gamut. Our coloring runs from the lightest of lights, to the darkest of darks; our hair textures run from bone straight to the tightest of curls; we are tall and short, skinny and voluptuous; freckles, clear, and troubled skins; from strikingly beautiful to okay looking; the sweetest of temperaments to the worse dispositions; well-educated to just barely knowledgeable; financially-challenged to insanely wealthy; from athletic to clumsy; and everything in between. We allow others to define what we should or should not look like, yet we have been overwhelming emulated by so many others. All other races see it; some envy it; and others have attempted to denigrate it. Stand up and be proud of who and what you are, because if you don't, no one else will. Because, you know what - Black is absolutely Beautiful, and we as a race, have cornered the markets of beauty, brains, and brawn.

CHAPTER 8
Psychological Warfare

If you ever pay attention to medical statistics, Black Americans hold the highest spot for almost every disease and illness known to man. We are at the top of any statistical scale for high blood pressure, diabetes, high cholesterol, heart failure, cancers, obesity, and, relatively speaking, academics. We constantly hear statistics, that indicate a trend towards everything negative, about being Black. The message is delivered in a way that speaks volumes, and of authority. The information routinely indicated that it is supported by hard facts.

Based on the Merriam-Webster definition of statistics, **Statistics** is a branch of mathematics dealing with the _collection_ (bringing things together), _analysis_ (a careful study), _interpretation_ (the way something is explained), _and presentation_ (activity in which someone shows, describes, or explains something), _of masses_ of numerical data.

 I'm okay with the information if the facts where statistically accurate for everyone, and not just a select neighborhood of people. And if our race is number one for almost every ailment known to man, what is it that Black Americans are doing that is so much more different than any other race? It cannot always be our diet because we all don't eat the same. It cannot be our environment because we all do not live the same. It cannot be our views on health, because we all do not approach health issues the same. We live where you live; eat what you eat; drink what you drink; work where you work; play where you play; and exercise where you exercise. Our actual bloodlines are so diluted that it is difficult to find a Black American that is 100% sub-Saharan. So, what could it be, and who is it behind all of the statistical facts?

Truth be told, if we are number one for so many illnesses and we are still living amongst the population, we are a more valuable resource to survival than anyone wants to admit, and a medical miracle by all standards. Instead of being extinct, we are surviving and thriving against all odds.

Please do not misinterpret what I have placed into print. I am not saying that Black Americans do not have health issues. Yes, we do. And I do not mean that we should ignore the reports. No, we should not. What I say to you is that, yes, there is a health crisis, but it is not just because we are Black Americans. The crisis is based on how our health issues are managed. Let me explain.

Black Americans have access to the same health care advantages as non-Blacks. The difference is the approach, reception, and administration.

We **approach** our health issues as though they are not our own. What I mean by that statement, is that if we experience a health problem, we immediately ignore it, or give the management of it to someone else.

The **reception** is that we immediately accept the first findings and take it as 'gospel'. We do not attempt to challenge them.

The **administration** is that we take whatever treatment is prescribed, without asking the most important questions pertaining to why. And we readily accept all medications because we believe that a pill will fix everything.

The number one thing for us as a race, is to realize that by ignoring a health problem, it will not go away. If you cannot afford to address the problem with a doctor, there are places that will help. And if it is a matter of cost, there are places that would assist with the finances. So, face the problem, quit making excuses, and take ownership of your health and the health of your loved ones.

Second, it *is* your health, so own it. What I mean by that statement is that, you are the one with the problem and you are the one that needs a solution. Take charge and be involve with your health management. Don't go to a doctor with the expectation of being fixed, without any participation from you. And if you are not satisfied with the findings by your doctor, go to another until your health problem is completely resolved. Don't settle for less.

Also, if you are given medication, investigate the prescription and its impact to you and your health.   You are not a 'lab rat' or a 'Guinea pig'. Don't accept that everything you receive from the medical community is in your best interest.

My son nearly cut his finger completely off. At the time, he was away at school. An 18-year-old freshman at college.   When he called me about the issue, I explained to him what he needed to do – rinse the wound, wrap it tight, and get to the emergency room. He did just that. When he returned to his dorm and called me, the second question I asked him was, "What type of medicine did you receive?" His response was, "Oxycodone. A bottle of 20 pills." My first thought was that, even though my son was on his own and away at college, he was still only 18 years of age. At that age, he cannot purchase tobacco products or alcohol but he can be given a strong opiate, without my consent. Does this make any sense? My response to him was to take one Advil©, go to bed, and for him to bring me the entire prescription the next day, after his last class. He did as I instructed. You see, I counted the entire bottle. I knew that he would do as I directed him to, but in counting the pills and as a mother, I needed that affirmation.

My purpose for mentioning this story is because prescriptions can be too freely given and too easily additive. If you need them, take them. But be realistic about taking them because they are still DRUGS.

Whether prescribed or not, drugs are still drugs, and you can become their slaves.

(Merriam-Webster describes a drug as something and often an illegal substance that causes addiction, habituation, or a marked change in consciousness.

 My 18-year-old son didn't need that prescription. The single dose of Advil© gave him the relief that he needed.

Wikipedia describes a drug as any substance (other than food that provides nutritional support) that, when inhaled, injected, smoked, consumed, absorbed via a patch on the skin, or dissolved under the tongue causes a physiological change in the body).

One of the biggest problems that we have is our easy acceptance of the first diagnosis that we receive. If it doesn't make any sense to you, then work to make it so that you understand. It's your health that you are dealing with and you need to make sure that everything you are told, and every prescription that you receive, is in your best interest. Invest in a Physician's Desk Reference Book – the PDR Pocket Guide to Prescription Drugs®. The book is about $7.99 and contains information pertaining to prescription drugs and their side effects, as well as counter-effects from the use of different drugs. The side effects and counter-effects are very important because, if you are prescribed one drug for one problem, it has the potential of a side effect that may triggering another more serious problem. The side effect can be severe enough that you may require another prescription. But, if you do not pay close attention to the warnings associated with each prescription, the two drugs that you have been prescribed may have the potential of an even more severe health problem. The PDR pocket guide is a great tool to have available, especially when you are prescribed multiple drugs.

Last but not least, make sure that your doctor is doing everything within their power to provide you with the best health care, possible. You are spending the same kind of money for the same type of health care, and you should never accept anything less. Get in there and get involved. Your health and well-being should not be based on your race or gender, but on you as a human-being. And don't be mad at you medical providers because they generalize in your health care. They basically generalize the health care for all of their patients. You specialize in your health care because it is your health that you are concerned for. Become more involved and take notice. And, don't believe that you don't have a problem just because there is no a history. History starts somewhere and it could very well start with you.

STEREOTYPES

Do you ever get tired of the fried chicken and collard green jokes? Why do people continue to make jokes about our big lips and big butts? And the watermelon jokes never seem to stop coming? I could go on but I won't because this is quite enough to start.

Well, I don't know about you, but I doubt that the chicken restaurant chains would continue to exist, if Blacks were the only ones eating chicken. And, have you bought a bunch of collard greens, lately? Their high prices are not because Blacks are the only ones consuming greens. Also, there are a lot of busy plastic surgeons who are making big money from lip and butt implants, and there are not that many black patients receiving them. Watermelon is being sold everywhere, and throughout the entire year. Are there enough Black Americans to sustain that type of supply?

These stereotypical comments, made about Black people are very old and tiresome. And though the comments continue, it indicates to me that, those who make these comments, do not really have much else to say. They laugh at each other's silly joke, and we bow down to the sarcasm and criticism.

Guess what, I like collard greens, watermelon, and chicken, and have no plans of stopping my consumption. And my big lips and fat butt are God-given assets, that didn't cost me one dime.

Airtime

Are you afraid to walk near a group of Black Teenagers? Do you intentionally cross the street if you see more than one Black person congregating? If you see a group of Blacks celebrating, do you wonder if they are involved in some type of gang activity? When you see a Black person driving a nice vehicle or living in a nice house, is your first thought that they got their gains via nefarious acts? If Blacks move into your nice neighborhood, do you think the neighborhood is on the decline? You may say that you don't but there are a lot of people who, rather consciously or subconsciously, think the worst. Yet, all other races are accepted with open arms. My husband and I moved into a quiet, unassuming neighborhood in Naperville, Illinois. After about a year of living there, one of our neighborhoods informed me that, when my husband and I moved into the neighborhood, they immediately expect the area to decline. She also stated that now, every time my husband would mow the lawn, her husband would mow their lawn, and she appreciated that.

In the military, I had a friend who let me know that he would never fly with this one pilot but he wouldn't even blink about flying with the other pilot. The first pilot was Black and the squadron commander. The second pilot was new daredevil lieutenant. My friend was also Black.

Some Blacks are steadfast in their belief that there are no Blacks in their economic or social levels, and they refuse to date or mate below their standards. This is a hard and fast rule for many people and they will not deviate from their beliefs. Yet, if the tables were flipped on them, and they become the economic and social piranha of the race, how would they feel then?

How many times have you watched the news reports about shootings and killings, robberies and muggings? If the culprit is Black, their picture is displayed immediately, but if the culprit is not Black, it takes some time before you even know who they are. The culprit could be your next-door neighbor who committed the crime. Unless that person is Black, you may never see their faces reported in the media. Also, when a Black person is sentenced for a crime, there is no compassion for our situation, even if this is our first offense. But others are looked upon as being innocent, yet caught up in the moment. Yes, many of the offenses we do own, but many are spurious charges that are exacerbated because of race.

When there is work to be done around your area, do you first consider every other race of people before you even look to your own? Is your first thought that Blacks are a lazy bunch of people, or that Blacks can't be trusted to do the work, correctly?

If you look at the media, if you talk with your friends, if you work in an environment where you are a serious minority, chances are you will feel the need to go along with the crowd and make negative comments about your own race, not realizing that **you are Black**, also. If you are talking about them, you are talking about yourself.

All of these things can equate to Psychological Warfare, and Black Americans contribute heavily to the negative ramifications of this. Think about it. We are no better than anyone else because we have been known to disparage the Black race, routinely.

We should do better with our own kind because if we can't, we should never expect anyone else to. We are stronger than that and most people realize this. Those that do not, don't count.

Don't play into the lies and stereotypes that depict Black Americans as a violent race of people. We are no more violent or destructive that any other race. We just allow the concept of negrophobia to exists by the actions of the few, and the inactions of the many.

CHAPTER 9
Lifestyle Changes

A lot of the health issues that we experience can be managed, or corrected completely, through lifestyle changes. Prepare your meals. You don't have to be the Next Top Chef or some Culinary Artist, to prepare your meals. Simple fare is good enough. And prepare your meals from scratch. If you can microwave a frozen TV dinner, you can turn on a stove top. And the meal will be better for you. Also, slow down on the fast food. Chances are that you do not know what is in the fast foods that you eat, but you would know what was in the meal that you prepared from scratch.

Ever wonder if processing of foods contributes to diabetes, Alzheimer's, Autism, some cancers? I'm old school and don't recall so many people experiencing so many powerful health issues. But I was also raised during an era when we prepared almost everything from scratch.

Better eating habits will do wonders for your health, but so will exercise. So, get moving! If you can make it to a fast food drive-up window, you can get up and walk around your neighborhood for a few minutes. You will be amazed at the results.

If your neighborhood is so bad that you cannot get outside of your door, there is another problem that you need to address. Get involved.

Address the issues with your elected officials. And if they are not willing to do their job, elect someone who will. If government leadership is effective in non-Black neighborhoods, then it should be just as effective in Black neighborhoods, but it takes the community to be involved. Quit talking yourself out of participating, and stop listening to others who discourage involvement. Don't say that you can't make a change and that no one will listen. If you can come together and march in protest of social issues, then you can come together for a better and safer neighborhood for you and your family. The power is in the unified voice, not the cowardly threat. Make the changes you need to better your environment, your health, and your family's well-being.

One last but very important comment. There is no reason why Black Americans should be on the bottom of the educational ladder. We are just as gifted, just as talented, just as academically able as any other race of people. We chose to accept what others say about our abilities or inabilities. A non-Black cannot describe why a Black person is lacking, on any issue. They can only tell you what they have observed and what is statistical.

If you don't learn, it's not because they say that you are not able to comprehend, it is because you chose not to comprehend. Ignorance and incompetence does not know race, creed, or gender. If you are ignorant and lacking knowledge, it is just you. There are too many highly intelligent Black people. You have the ability to be within the group. Apply yourself and prove others wrong. Prove yourself wrong. If the resources are not available to you, work with what you have. If your school does not make the effort to ensure that you have what you need to get educated, file complaints with the school board. Get your local NAACP Chapter involved. Let others know what the true struggles are that your school faces so that they can assist where you cannot. There are many organizations that are available to help, but they can only do so if they are made aware that their help is needed.

Get your local government involved, and if they don't want to provide any assistance, go to the state, and the federal governments. Get rid of those who refuse to provide assistance and elect new representatives. Contrary to the belief of people like Donald Trump, there are those of us who dutifully pay our taxes so that everyone gets a fair share of the support needed to grow and survive.

One important note – when you fight for funding to support academics and your community, ensure that the resources do not get re-directed to communities that are already excelling. This would defeat the purpose.

Quit complaining that you can't get what you need. Step up and get involved. No one will bring it to you, you have to go and get it for yourself. We are a proud race of people, but sometimes pride and arrogance can be a detriment to success. Remember that **Pride** is directly related to conceit; and **Arrogance** is confidence out of control.

CHAPTER 10

Laws on the Books/Are they in your Best Interest

We tend to believe that we are protected by Laws that govern our country. There are some laws that do indeed, protect us but there are still many laws that were always designed, and still exist to negate the rights of Blacks. Because each state may develop their own local laws, policies, and procedures, we tend to miss them until the opportunity to use them, transpires. That is not the time to realize that the rights and freedoms that you thought you had, does not exist because of your race, creed, or gender.

The United States of America is a country of some of the brightest minds in the world. And many Black Americans are definitely grouped among the best of the brightest minds. Do we use them to advance our culture, or do we work diligently to self-promote? Do we even consider the possibility of the damage some laws may create for our race? We don't even consider taking the time to review the laws, until it is too late. We get caught in the traps.

There is probably an enormous amount of outdated laws on the books that should have been removed a long time ago. They become difficult to challenge when we are before a judge and jury. And Black Americans have a more difficult time with our defense, than most.

Chapter 10

We need to look at these laws; we need to work together to review their effectiveness and relevance; and we need to work diligently to remove the ones that are so outdated, that their relevance may predate the Civil Rights era, or even as far back as slavery. As a race, working to correct these antiquated laws will be in our best interest. If you don't believe that they exist, consider the 'one-drop rule' before you make that error in judgment.

We, as a race, put a lot of energy in marches and protests. They can be very effective, and even result in significantly, positive changes in our favor. But there is another way that protesting can be just as effective, and the effects can be permanent. Review the laws and codes

> per Wikipedia, the one-drop rule is a social and legal principle of racial classification that was historically prominent in the United States, asserting that any person with even one ancestor of sub-Saharan-African ancestry ("one drop" of black blood) is considered Black (Negro in historical terms

that directly impact the livelihood of Black Americans; work with the government to remove the ones that should have been removed in the last century; and improve on the ones that are outdated with facts. We are a powerful race of people but our hands will always be tied by the laws that bind us all, if we do not correct the rules that hold us back from enjoying the fruits of our labor.

If you ever notice, most racial conflicts in this country, are black and white. The silent protest parade in New York City about the East St. Louis riots of 1917, and the marches during the 1950's and 60's, are two examples of how Blacks have always march against injustice. Other races of people were on the sidelines, waiting to see the results, and yet they benefited from either side's progress. No matter what the negative issues are, if we work hard to correct the disparaging laws on the books that keep our race from moving ahead, we help others, as well.

One of the things that I have learned about Black Americans is that, we know how to survive and we will thrive, and bigotry and hatred will only strengthen our cause.

When my ancestors were forced to cross that **MIDDLE PASSAGE** against their will; to journey to a place they had no knowledge of; to

per Encyclopædia Britannica: **Middle Passage**, the forced voyage of enslaved Africans across the Atlantic Ocean to the New World.

be separated from family and familiar surroundings forevermore; to be treated as less than livestock by their captors; enslaved to the capriciousness of men who did not have the strength of mind and body to do their own labors; to be beaten and slaughtered for any inadequacies including breathing too loudly; Black America has survived. Yet, after all that our ancestors had suffered and continued to suffer through, even after slavery was supposedly ended, and what our race has been going through since then, we still cannot catch a break in 2017. For any group of people to believe that after over four hundred years of overt and covert racism, Black Americans still have not earned the right to be left alone, to enjoy the fruits of our labor, that only indicates to me that that group of people fear what we have become - an unstoppable force to be reckoned with. Their fears are giving us more power than we know. In this case, fear is a 'double-edged' sword. There are many who are working hard to ensure the extinction of the Black American race. But they forget that for centuries, Black Americans have subconsciously and successfully, worked just as hard to ensure that we do not become **ANOTHER ENDANGERED SPECIES.**

www.ingramcontent.com/pod-product-compliance
Lightning Source LLC
Chambersburg PA
CBHW070818240726
48654CB00007B/395